Craniotomy Sestinas

Craniotomy Sestinas

Poems by

Leonard Kress

Cover design by Shay Culligan
Detail from *The Extraction of the Stone of Madness,* a painting by
Hieronymus Bosch depicting trepanation

ISBN: 978-1-952326-72-1

Kelsay Books
502 South 1040 East, A-119
American Fork, Utah, 84003

Acknowledgments

Harvard Review: "Eradicating the Rodent"

Connecticut Poetry Review: "Polish Oratorio"

The Incredible Sestina Anthology: "Miss New Jersey"

Philadelphia Stories: "Under the El Tracks, "Barefoot"

McSweeney's Online: "The Seven Signs"

Matter: "Free Mumia Cheesesteaks"

Solstice: "Blue Grass (with Homage to Louis Zukofsky)" "Sestina
    with a Line from Major Jackson's Reverse Voyager"

The Body: "Pomeranians"

Gulf Stream: "Fish"

Fruita Pulp: "Rigoletto," "House on Ashbourne Road," "Wetting
    the Bed," "Crossing Over"

Corium Review: "Clavdia Chaucat's Chest X-ray," "Monsieur
    Proust Takes a Walk"

Hinchas des Poesia: "Craniotomy"

Valparaiso Poetry Review: "Songlines"

Ginger Bread Review: "Cyclops in Love"

Scoundrel Time: "My 6th Grade Teacher"

Chaleur Journal: "The Book of the Wilderness," "Whitmania"

Passager: "1968"

Verse-Virtual: "Faust Dancing"

Map Literary: "Flower Hospital," "Rasadeva Dance," "The Middle
    Ages"

Some of these poems appeared in limited edition chapbooks on
Seven Kitchens Press and Moonstone Books

Contents

Always midway between design and anecdote. "The significant images of myth, the materials of the bricoleur, are elements which can be defined by two criteria: they have had a use, as words a piece of discourse which mythical thought 'detaches' in the same way as bricoleur, in the course of repairing them, detaches the cogwheels of an old alarm clock; and they can be used again either for the same purpose or for a different one if they are at all diverted from their previous function"
—*La Pensée sauvage,* Claude Levi-Strauss

*

He searches out the wisdom of all the ancients,
And busies himself with prophecies;
He observes the discourse of famous men,
And penetrates the intricacies of the figure…
He searches out the hidden meaning of proverbs.
—*Wisdom of Sirach 39*

*

"He had to know all the tribes and families, all the tribal elders, all place-names and events. He had to be thoroughly familiar with all questions of the time. Ready wit and resource, the ability to give quick answers—these were accomplishments without which the *akyn* found no popular esteem.

Further, he must have sang-froid. Even when he was jeered and when mockery was heaped upon him he must always remain calm. He might not, moreover, intoxicate himself with others' melodies, he must have a voice of his own, and must measure the earth with his own poetry. His every word must hit the mark like a dagger thrust. Nor might he feign emotion that he did not feel; he must take the words from his heart as water is taken from the source."
from *Mein Leben* by the Kazakh epic poet, Dzhambul.
—*A Poet's Glossary,* Edward Hirsch

Craniotomy

The surgeon drilled a hole into my skull
and cut away a flap of bone to reach
inside, where he could then excise the mass
that grew, unchecked. My chart said nothing
about the nature of the growth—thought
become flesh, momentarily exposed to the air.

I think of the French poet Guillaume Apollinaire,
injured in the First World War, his skull
trepanned, who afterwards thought
only of the death of beauty. It's quite a reach
comparing my ordeal to his—nothing
like an exploding Axis shell—my mere benign mass.

I never brought cubism to the masses,
never tried to steal the *Mona Lisa,* like Apollinaire,
who implicated Picasso, which came to nothing.
All before the doctors cracked open his skull,
so it might be quite a reach
to posit that his poems and thoughts

had been usurped. That is what I thought,
though, and still think, that the removed mass
was functional, and it's not an act of overreach
to wonder what's been lost. Of course I did not air
my grievance to the surgeon who split my skull—
to him, the radiologist, the lab, it was nothing

but extraneous meat and vessels. But this *nothing,*
I submit, was a sort of incarnation, thought
transubstantiated to cells sheltered within the skull.
And it shouldn't surprise that I use language of the Mass.
Where else but in a sestina can I air
my inane theories hoping they might reach

sympathetic ears? It's taken decades to reach
this point, to acknowledge that I am nothing
if a muse does not seek refuge from the open air
and implant—and thus displace—thought.
That entity the surgeon called *mass*
was really a grotto ensconced inside my skull.

Eradicating the Rodent

Picasso said to Braque, I see a squirrel
in your painting, there among the table top
items—tobacco pouch, pipe, etc. No,
said Braque, until he looked again;
he was, after all, a formalist
in control of what the viewer does and does not see.

Now that you mention it, I can't *not* see
it there. Annoying rodent, haplessly squirreled
away in mind, cracking the formalist's
nut. Picasso, was, of course, at the top
of his game, and had nothing to lose or gain
if someone spotted a penguin where no

bird was, in an etching, say, of two blue figures we know
are alone, with a heel of bread, some wine. We could see
the interloper and laugh again,
as *now we see it/now we don't.* He could kill the squirrel
if it twitched its nose, bring down his brush hard on the top
of its skull. Those silly, gutless, control-freak formalists

got it all wrong. But what happens when formal
coherence is attempted in an abstract composition. No
need to explain or eradicate. A spinning top
appears, let it twirl, as long as you want to see
it, spin along, watch for its bite, but feed the squirrel,
and after losing yourself in dots & swirls & shapes, look again

to see them transformed. A jazz musician gains
your trust by introducing a well-known form
of a melody, seizing it, mocking it, then squirrelly
letting it dissolve into the chord changes. He knows
that we know, just as the painter will see
what we see, and each time it's like taking it from the top,

once more, like a simple gift, cherry on the top
accidental, momentary, stage front, dropped again
to foment desire. Don't you see
how it works? How formalism
abhors a vacuum, that there should be no
need for eradication. Look, gone in a flash, that squirrel.

Faust Dancing

The only time I danced in a ballet,
I was already old, at least too old to appear
on stage in tights. I was taking a class,
not my first, culminating in a performance,
15 weeks of frappé, dégagé, at the barre
followed by chaîné, assemblé in the center.

I was never comfortable being the center
of attention, you'd think I'd avoid ballet,
that my masculine-American sense would bar
me from that realm. Oh, I could claim appearance
is not reality, that I relished performing
behind the girl in the backless leotard, in class

to improve her volleyball spikes, or that the class
was good exercise a way to center
myself—all about balance and focus. We performed
a dance from Charles Gounod's Faust ballet,
and from the audience reaction it would appear
that I, lone male among females, for 100 bars,

held my own. Afterwards, I stopped by a bar
for a beer, several, a working class
establishment and marvelled at the appearance
and sudden disappearance of a throbbing in the center
of my chest when the three-quarter time music of the ballet
edged out the jukebox grind, as my inner organs performed

ecstatically. It would have been quite a performance
if the dart-tossing couples or the hot bar-
tender weren't distracted by the basketball ballet
leaping dunk on the large screen. I tell my classes
that Greek philosophers always aim for the center,
that Kant is a brilliant fanatic, that appearance

always undermines reality, that empiricists appear
to be reasonable but are not, that truth is performative,
that Yeats was right—the center
cannot hold and nothing we can do will bar
the beast from bearing down upon us. My class
is popular, but my students would learn more from ballet.

Stairway of Farewells

after the painting by Giacomo Balla

They hesitate on the stairs,
all three women, poised as if to wave
back to the place where they came from, their descent
well underway. One grips the rail
and smiles, as does another, stylish in red,
hem spilling into her past and future.

The third figure in this painting (by the not-yet-Futurist
Balla) sacked in black, winded from the stairs,
must lean against the wall. Her face is red,
burning through her mourning. She waves
her fitter cohorts on, prayerful that the rail
is there to guide her slow descent

down into the open air of her neighborhood, a descent
that led her through an oscillating vortex of future
loss that she no longer has the strength to rail
against. The younger others smile and keep staring
back, though soon they'll both be riding the wave,
veiled hats bobbing on the crest, down into the blood-red

depths. It is, I suppose, the shyer one, the one in red
who won't return, whose anticipated descent
will seem to the other abduction, and her arms will wave
like a ululating voice, unconvinced the future
will return her daughter. The pause, then, on these stairs
seems calculated to derail

the story—all those perspective lines like rail-
road tracks that vanish in a distance. We've already read
the ending time and again. The ending that makes my stare
fix them in a gaze that will not halt descent,
and will not change a future
determined by the picture plane. Only a *New Wave*

that submerges vanishing points, a wave
as twisted as the stairway with its serpentine rail,
will (as Balla was to later know) fix the future
in the present—innocent as the girl in red
who stretches out her visit into the long descent,
even when she takes, two at a time, the stairs.

Polish Oratorio

I was tutoring the son and daughter of the great composer.
conversational English for her, literature for him;
together we struggled to bring *Howl* into Polish
served tea & cakes by a poor relative
who also raked leaves, tended steaming pots, and read
romances in the corner. No one felt guilt

in this grand manor by the Byzantine Church with its gilt
cupolas. Moravian wine and chocolates—gifts for the composer
delivered daily. Baltic herring, Egyptian reeds
for his son's oboe. It was rumored the government feared him
more than shipyard workers in Gdansk. All is relative
when it comes to revolution, the authorities polish

their image by letting him have what few Polish
citizens have. State of War. Show trials. Guilt.
foreign investment. Nostalgia. Plum-jobs for relatives—
it all unfolds in front of us, while the composer
composes in Paris. And who can blame him—
sycophants, students, impresarios, no time to read

the Warsaw papers. His latest piece, reed-
heavy and trenchant, its libretto rife with Polish
romantic tropes. Everyone expects great things from him.
I must be the only one who feels guilt
around here. The daughter's composition
book is full of backwards writing. Alina, her country relative

burns husks outside and wax effigies from other relatives
for the *Day of the Dead* celebration. I've read
about her gap-toothed smile (mark of Venus—composer
of love) in medieval astrologies. Soviet mascara, nail polish,
quick to shed tears, but ardent in desire and guilt-
free. Everyone, including me, in awe of him.

His early symphonies expound Eastern Orthodox hymns,
basso profundo replaced by strings that question relative
pitch. Taking on the West's unbridled guilt
over Hiroshima and Auschwitz. The rampaging Red
army killing fields and forests, a generation of Polish
professors, priests, and poets lost. Revived in his composition.

Barefoot

When I was younger, I was always leaving my shoes
behind, always, though, with a good excuse.
One time, the March on Washington to protest
the bombing of Cambodia, Kent State, after settling down
for the night in a church loft, awakened
from sleep to romp on the Capitol lawn to play hide

and seek by the Doric columns, someone hid
my things. For the entire weekend I went shoe-
less. The grassy mall, Joan Baez—we had awakened
the planet's consciousness, it seemed, the Pentagon had no excuse
not to implode, its walls tumbling down,
its frayed-suit denizens joining the earnest frolic in protest

of themselves and their deeds. An idea they'd surely protest.
It happened so often my soles resembled hides,
thick, calloused, impenetrable. So it was easy to amble down
the chunk gravel path by the Wissahickon without shoes,
side-stepping horseshit with friends, excused
from their lack of hardiness, though clearly awake

to the chance I might be on to something, in the wake
of others who'd gone barefoot before. They don't protest
as we pay homage to *Chief Tedyuscung's* statue (poor excuse
for heroic sculpture: the last of his tribe, nowhere to hide,
gazing west and chiseled naked, not even shoes
for protection—from smashed beer bottles flung down

from the summit. Once when I felt the need to calm down,
ready for some sort of awakening
I found a huge zazen session, removed my shoes
and entered the campus gym, ignoring protesting
locked-out gymnasts. I tried to hide
the fire blazing in my knees, having to excuse

myself, barefoot again, for what seemed an excuse
of a counseling session. Winter was bearing down,
and the smug, bored psychologist could not hide
her diagnosis. When YAHWEH woke
up Moses to propose his mission, wary Moses protested,
but still approached sacred ground, removing first his shoes.

Braids

According to the Talmud, God braided
Eve's hair for her wedding. He served
as Adam's groomsman, too, though I doubt
he made any *ball & chain* jokes—before the Fall
at least....And yes, if they had a garden
wedding, there must have been a steamy wedding night—

every position given a made-up name that endless night
by Adam, with Eve's input, of course. He unbraided
her hair slowly, as if each strand was a garden
snake released, there not to destroy but to serve
the cause of love, the abyss they so easily fell
into. The Talmud expresses no doubt

about this. Put aside all those doubts
about immodesty, decency, lady-of-the night
attire and fashion, the judgment that will fall
upon you, if you adorn yourself or braid
your hair. You do not serve
that master, who never halted mid-day in the garden

to note the sunlight dripping through the garden
leaves, splashing over, eradicating doubt
that this moment is in the service
of all others. That this night
beginning with two tight French braids
which swing in the breeze and fall

effortlessly down her back and will fall
along with her to the damp garden
floor. And the tips of those braids,
curling like question marks of doubt
will soon unravel—a way to prolong the night.
I remember, when we first met, how undeserving

I felt in her presence, how all nature served
our cause and how quickly I fell
in love, perhaps that very night
as we strolled, sloshing through the village gardens,
flooded that summer. The one thing I didn't doubt,
as I touched and took in the bound-in scent of her braids.

On the Beach

We spend the whole day at the Lake Erie beach,
cranes and gulls, pulverized shells. Two families with kids,
avoiding the odd discarded syringe—*No, you can't*
go in that water! But they do, wading through wetlands
to plunge in, while the husbands discuss the ethics
of launching the war. Disobedience without fallout—

splash, dunk. One mother's nursing breasts almost fall out
of her suit as she joins the spray. Back on the beach
the one who isn't her husband drops the Ethics
text he reads, gazing at *them,* after he hears one of the kids
shriek in what could be pain. The wetlands
glister under the sun. It is mere cant,

he figures. Returning, momentarily to Kant's
Categorical Imperative. What about the radioactive fallout
from the Nuclear Plant looming in the wetlands,
closed twice this season, as was the beach
for high e-coli counts—how safe are the kids,
the other husband anguishes. How ethical

are they, as parents, exposing…Damn the Ethics
of monogamy, they all think, why can't
we just do what we want? After all, our kids
are too young to note—no serious fallout
likely. Disappear further down the beach,
better yet, that bird blind in the wetlands

free from birders now. These wetlands,
ordinarily flocked with them and their ethical
binoculars and field guides—a hunter on this beach
wouldn't survive. Sadly, our families can't
stay past dark. Shoes shaken, though what falls out
is gritty and sharp and all the kids

complain and whine—our darling kids
who brought us together but keep us apart. The wet landing
of mini-van seats, strapped in so no one falls out
of the rightful place. Today the ethicist
gets a pass—Duty prevails over Pleasure. Kant
is pleased, but he's not exploring that same beach.

Miss New Jersey

I almost dated Miss New Jersey
once. No, this is not the punch line
to some joke. And it didn't happen
decades after the pageant when she'd become
unrecognizable as such. Maybe just a year
or two after her title, her sash still pressed

and unboxed. However, if I were pressed
I wouldn't divulge whether or not the jersey
came off—but I admit, *it was a very good year*
for small town girls...at least that was the song line
we heard in a bar one night after we became
friends. Good for me, too, if it happened

that her scumbag boyfriend left—which didn't happen,
of course. She couldn't resist his full-court press,
against spilled blood and Casinos, what would become
of him, if she left New Jersey,
where she substitute-taught junior high music, in line
for full-time, if she stuck it out a year,

teaching steelworkers' sons and daughters. The year
she won, she toured military bases and happened
to appear with Bob Hope, even became the punch line
of his suggestive jokes, while he pressed
up close. Vietnam, I thought, but it might've been Jersey's
Fort Dix. She didn't dare sing (fearing she'd become

a laughingstock) the Schubert song, *Bliss,* which became
pageant legend. Instead, for *Mr. Hope,* it was the year's
hit, *Tie a Yellow Ribbon,* which played well in Jersey.
Though after a single tour, it happened:
she lost her will to sing and nothing could press
her into it. Time after time, her rehearsed line

was "God took my voice," and with that I drew the line
on taking things further. For she was becoming
sorrowful (a different Schubert song) and depressed.
Her inability to sing lasting almost a year.
Then she sang *Bliss* for me—I don't know how it happened—
right before she moved away from New Jersey.

Under the El Tracks

The thing I so clearly remember
from the years we lived beneath the el tracks,
or just blocks from them, were the freezing
waits for the train and the hopelessly long
walks through the neighborhoods—Harrowgate,
Torresdale, Fishtown, the bums and crosswalk prophets

we'd encounter. Always the same, *What will it profit
a man if he gains the whole world*...I remember
encountering one preaching outside the shut gate
of a half-demolished *art-deco* theater. He tracked
our arrival, our baby strolled deep into her long
afternoon nap, questioned our wisdom—letting her freeze

like this. My wife with her camera busily freezing
the twisted steel beams, drooping finials, scenes a prophet
might relish, beads of gilt debris melted in the long
midnight of fires, crack, and rats. What we won't remember
in the rush to rebuild. This was the place beneath the tracks
where prostitutes sheltered all winter, their gate-

way to cruising cars, one by one, with that skirt-hiking gait,
raising 5 or 10 fingers, like figures in an ancient Chaldean frieze.
Everyone takes them in, walkers, drivers, passengers on the track-
less trolley—you might wonder if they're the harlots the prophet
Ezekiel railed against: Oholah and Oholibah as they remember
their Egyptian lovers, whose members were as long

as those of horses, those sisters longed
for the orgies of their youth, before the city shut its gate
to them. Those officers with girded loins they remembered
even in exile, even in the heat of this deep freeze.
They crowded around, cooing over the baby—the prophet
wasn't paying attention—losing track

of time, and money to be made under the el tracks.
It seems they've been doing this for so long
you'd think they know: Forget the prophet
Ezekiel's rant—listen to Isaiah instead. *Enter the gates*
of the city. Take your harps and sweet songs. Don't freeze,
sing that you may be remembered.

In the Beskidy Mountains of Southern Poland

Where am I now, this town with the shifting border—
Poland, Austria, the Czech Republic? Could
it be the Ottoman Empire? If I join the children's
hopscotch chalked on cobblestones, spin round,
dip down to snatch the gleaming coin, whose face
might smudge—Habsburg, Hus, Piast, Suleiman the Magnificent?

The only thing that matters here is magnificent
lukewarm beer waitresses slosh in front of the boarders,
far from village wives, after-shift miners with coal-bin faces.
One of them hugs me, then another, shifting to holds that could
kill if I don't escape, slipping behind one waitress, around
another—whose hip-heisting moves turn them to bawling children,

weeping songs about Linden trees and lies, children
orphaned by the last war. Outside I spot the magnificent
remains of the Habsburg tower and climb the round
stairs, breathless, to search for forbidden borders.
I'd behave like some Franz-Joseph protégé if I could,
as I stake out the barefoot girl whose face

I'm sure I've seen before. She's on the Polish side, facing
the Czech, the tortuous path leading away from childhood,
urging her lazy cow on and on. If she could,
she'd cease tugging its chain, let its magnificently
bulging udders sway and drag in the dust, the borders
of cruelty. If she did, though, I'd find, as she'd round

the bend, the message its udders script, stay around
to read them—like a polygraph expert—and face
the truth. *Yes.* (I'll meet you in that Linden grove by the border,
you can slip your fingers in my braid the way children
do, to urge the strands apart.) Or, *No*. Magnificent
as that sounds, there's no way those kids could

have tossed that coin, a money-changer did, so he could
clear his pocket for dollars. The tower spins round,
out of control, dizzying, there's nothing magnificent
about history here, where it gushes forth from each face.
I should climb down, head home, and raise children,
see just how possible it is to live on that border.

Cyclops in Love

Everyone's trying to get into the act,
but who would have expected an ugly beast
like him to croon like a Latin lover?
His eye winking tearfully, such a deep unexpected blue,
his fierce engorged head bent over
to elicit sympathy, his matted body,

kneeling in proposal, less massive than anybody
would have guessed. An almost elegant act,
pleading his case, his fertile land spreading over
two hillsides, sheep and goats galore, not the beast
you've heard about. She sits dreaming by the blue
sea, barely attentive, her heart set on a different lover,

a young shepherd bent on pursuing her. *Love
in her eyes sits playing,* he'd sing, seeing her body
barely covered, imagining the rest—an operatic blues,
perhaps, by Handel, right in the first act
when all is fun and games, before the percussive beast
appears. It's Cyclops, raging, melting, burning all over:

*Don't think me unsightly, a lamb has wool all over,
birds have plumage, trees have leaves, surely a lover
of them can love me. If I were a just a beast
could I offer you plums and cherries? Everybody
envies my shaded dells and groves—why do you act
like I'm not worth your time?* Still she blew

him off, remarked his one eye was not nearly as blue
as claimed, and waved her shepherd boy over—
hesitant until it's clear in the final act,
he faces competition. Now he's the arch-lover,
and she swoons and spreads for him, entire body
opening. She will never ever allow the beast

this access, and yes, this is the place where any beast
would grab a rock, not stopping at black and blue,
in wild agonized rage, to smash at least one body.
A satisfying end? We should, perhaps, think this over.
Cyclops, seeing such fervent, such feral love-
making in this version, disappears into the act.

20 Below

We drove the VW Bug up into the mountains,
five of us, two couples and me, a tag-along,
stalling out twice, after dark, deep in State
Game Land. It was on record the coldest
February ever. We made it to the hunting
cabin through sheer luck, a plowed stretch

of road. And flopped on cots, stretched
out in exhaustion and gratitude to the mountain
gods who blessed our entrance. We had no hunting
gear, no snowshoes, skis or even parkas along
with us, nothing but kerosene fumes to fight cold.
Except our leader, of course, whose downstate

cousins owned the cabin, maintained its primitive state
because they were Old Order Amish not wanting to stretch
their ways too far, and understood the cold
to be morally bracing, and the mountain
humbling. Our leader, whose family failed to play along
had been shunned years before, and only hunting

remained. He insisted that back home they'd hunt
him down, curse his apostasy, the black state
of his soul. Up here, though, they made sure to get along,
snowmobiled over to hawk meth and pot and stretch
their necks to gape at the girls. Away from the mountains,
back in the lush home meadows, one of them was a stone cold

Elder, wife and six kids, two black buggies and a cold
spring to envy, that is, if all hints of envy hadn't been hunted
down and flayed. My friends and I went up to the mountain,
making our own path, we wanted to escape the current state
of mind. And our leader, in mukluks and long johns stretched
over his hands and feet, leaped a small gorge leaving us a long

way off. We thought we might all get along
better without him—daring a romp in the cold,
when suddenly his girlfriend folded, fell stretched
out in a snowdrift, beseeching us not to hunt
for help. She had found, she said, oblivion, her desired state,
like her hero, the hero of Thomas Mann's *The Magic Mountain.*

Flower Hospital

You might think this hospital
contains a healing ward for injured flowers,
a quiet damp sunny place for them to recover
from mower blades and weed-whackers and mites,
from trampling boots and sprayed-on poisons,
a place where their growth could be aided and assisted

by dedicated staff. Instead it houses an Assisted
Living Center, abutting the hospital
wing, where old people, not yet fully poisoned
by their own meds, watch TV, re-pot flowers
and wander haplessly around. They might
thinks it's not forever, but they won't recover

as aides struggle to cover and re-cover
their shivering limbs and assist
them in the bathroom. And they might
express gratitude to those workers and hospital
volunteers, but they don't. The flowers
left by their bedsides could be poison

fairy tale apples. But it's them who embody the 3 poisons
identified by the Buddha—who assured recovery—
Delusion. Craving. Hostility. Right before his *Flower
Sermon,* wordless and mute, meant to assist
his over-thinking disciples, minds too hospitable
to conceptual thought, who, given the chance, might

try to deify him, rather than gathering all their might
to pay attention to their own minds. And the poisons
accumulating therein. Perhaps a hospital
is the best place to examine sickness and recovery
and how to do it without assistance,
the way bushes, trees, even flowers

repair themselves or perish. It is this flowering
the Buddha endorses. Even a mite
has a *Buddha Nature.* Assist
by doing no harm, and you eradicate the poison
in yourself, and thus you recover
yourself—leaving shed husks and petals in the hospital.

Bruno

Bruno Schulz, the Polish-Jewish writer
from a town buried deep in the Ukraine
taught art at the local high school, and in his spare
time painted his most obscene fantasies.
Mostly his own glib face on the body
of dwarfish, half-human creatures, creeping

at the feet of gorgeous pouting ladies. And to creep
out everyone, he sometimes depicted his writer
friends that way. Even his wife's naked body
showed up posed with prostitutes. Neighbors would crane
their necks to watch the couple pass. Fantasies
abounded in pre-war Central Europe—nothing spare

about them. The greatest, the Holocaust, did not spare
Schultz's life: a pair of feuding Nazi creeps
shot him in the street to bring about their Jew-free fantasy
world. He would have been the greatest writer
since Kafka, but prodigiously provincial Ukraine
let it all go—the notebooks, the drafts, the dead body,

all but small two books, a meager body
of work, which should cause us to despair
if it weren't so good, should cause us to crane
before resorting to art to stave off creeping
juggernauts. And yet, as Schultz in a letter wrote
to a friend, the only world that exists is fantasy,

for me, only life redeemed though fantastic
beauty has worth. If not, it is morally vapid, a body
decomposing, a living hell. Only material for writing
or paint....otherwise not worth sparing.
Is it worthwhile, then, to let this notion creep
in, hoist up as with a slow and steady crane

into our practice? To wade like the melancholy crane
hoarse screech and all, migratory fantasy
intact, into the marsh, dip into the creep,
bill latched onto to some pierced, mangled body—
dying parent, tortured child, to know that only unsparing
documentation of suffering will make you a writer.

Swanee River

My mother dragged me—whenever she shopped
for clothes, most often at Chatlins, a private
department store (the name's important, or else
I wouldn't mention it). There were mannequins,
a terrifying phalanx of them, headless and white
donning panties, girdles, and bras. I'd retreat

to a free-standing display case, an eye-level treat
for my 7-year old self, ignored by shoppers.
I'd pull a lever, a banjo strummed and a white
puppet in blackface, Barbie-sized, my own private
minstrel show, this gangly, flapping, manikin
dancing in his own glass cage. Spellbound—what else

could I do? Too entranced to smash the glass or else
mangle the gears. He could not escape, no retreat
behind the ranks of lascivious mannequins
blocking me from dressing rooms and stripped shoppers
embattled and secreted in their own private
mirrored display, the lights piercing and white.
The puppet only sang *Swanee River* by white
composer Stephen Foster. (Of course—why else
mention it.) Back home, in my private
world, I knew this song from daily retreats
into the Fireside Book of Songs, shopping
for a voice but voiceless as a mannequin,

my heart turning, ever seeking a man akin
to this one, able to overcome the white
noise around him, the nitpicky shoppers
threatening to take their business else—
where if the salesclerks didn't treat
them with due deference. In his own private

domain, among officers, a buck private,
his song could animate mannequins,
lead melancholy on a slow retreat
past the ignominious banks of any white
river, and raise a solitary voice, or else,
instill within me, grief and lament, among shoppers.

Proverbs 7 as if Written by the Roman Poet Propertius

I spied him spying on me from the window of his house,
peeking through the lattice, as I began to cross
the street, heading over to *her* place.
The sun just setting—darkness to provide cover
quickly. I didn't have long to wait
for her to emerge, her long hair like a heavy curtain

veiling her face, though he knew—inching his curtain
aside, exactly who she was. He knew her house
and those who dwelled inside. He sighed as if a weight
was simultaneously placed across
his chest and removed. He hopes that I'll discover
his right, that her unprovoked ambush might place

me in the role of *mugged or victim or prey,* will displace
the blame from me to her. Draw the curtain,
old man. You can judge a book by its cover.
This isn't the first time I've stopped by her house
cruising the neighborhood, pretending to cross
the street, if spotted. One can only wait

so long before the waiting
becomes its own sad game. But it won't replace
this bustling and restive ache that cuts across
all categories of good and evil like a curtain
call that is certain to bring the house
down. Understand, she doesn't care that her cover

will be blown. She has decked her bed with covers
of dyed Egyptian linen. Her embraces will have the weight
of sprinkled myrrh and aloe. Her husband is out of the house
for now, and she invites me to take his place.
So what if it is, as the cartoons say, *Curtains!*
For us, old man, the ultimate double-cross.

Once her path began to cross
mine, there was everything to discover
and nothing that any sort of curtain
could keep hidden, nothing that might lay in wait,
nothing that could ever take its place
in this or any other possible house.

Fish

Why does everything come back to fish?
The time of year when the Maumee River
is flush with human jetties, casters, waist-deep
in the chill, arms like pistons, their manic Spring quest
for Walleye insatiable. The catch won't be served
for dinner, though—fear of poisoning their young.

Turn to the musings of Carl Jung
to make sense of synchronicity, his take on fish,
beginning with a human-aquatic figure that served
as an ancient alchemical inscription. On the river
bank he encountered a giant creature in its quest
to reach water, only to disappear in the deep.

That same day, he saw a patient, in deep
despair, recount terrifying dreams she had as a young
girl, and her whole adult life had become a quest
to make sense of those giant nightmare fish
that continued to haunt her. Later, at a cafe on the river,
he savoured freshly caught rainbow trout served

by a waiter named Fischel. In dreams, the archetype serves
as stand-in for libido or greed; or if it's deep
in the sea—unconscious urges; if it leaps out of a river
then fright or redemption. When I was young,
hard as I tried, I was never able to hook a fish.
Though I did set out on various quests,

or set forth (into the dark wood) to use language of quest,
to find the exact cause I was meant to serve.
I knew of the Grail and the aged, wounded Fisher
King from Weston's *Ritual to Romance,* I was deep
in *The Psychology of Transference* by Jung.
I kept my implacable sense that this river

(and all rivers like it) was the River
separating the living from the dead, the quest-
ioner from the question, and that while I was young,
I had to dive in, for everything's a matter of serving
or being served. And how to approach the deep
recessed pools of the incorporeal, commanding fish.

Neo-Platonic Text as if Written by Wallace Stevens

Why does she sing at the mouth of my cave,
where I sit like one sentenced by Plato,
stolid and dully content with the light
that is not light but mimicking shadow,
where I find comfort in my sluggish despair
fiercely unable to gladden my sorrow.

I hear a voice so full of sorrow,
the sound of which bores in my bones a cave
that drains the marrow and sucks-in despair
banishable from the ideal world of Plato,
as nothing more than reflected shadow
distantly removed from the source of light.

Everything eternally longs for light,
and pines away as if in sorrow,
wanting to escape the unreal shadow.
Who'd choose to inhabit a musky cave,
aging and cranky, sober mock-Plato?
Who, right-minded would opt for despair?

Her singing intensifies my despair.
Sound that will not fall to the ground—so light
they flee in retreat. Ideally Plato
would not even allow the song's sorrow
existence beyond the stone of the cave,
for every song is still a heard shadow.

You would be scorched if a tree's shadow
did not block the sun, prevent the despair
of seething inside one's apartment cave,
reading out the days by electric light,
too trapped in thought to bear her sorrow,
not living, just reading books by Plato.

Her song, I'm sure, would move even Plato,
and the shape of her that casts a shadow
would tempt anyone away from sorrow
and make him hate the cause of his despair,
the cause so gravitous becoming light,
like echoed whistles heard in a cave.

The Book of Jezebel

Return to your wilds, Elijah. Go back to those stones
you lord over. Cough up a mantleful of prophecies
under the broom tree, while you sweep the crows' leavings.
Do you think your god can turn our fields
to dust? When my Ba'alite priests shed blood
into furrows and your own brothers storm the gates

to Asherah's love jades? Their limping gait
gives them away—cocks as hard as stones,
as they dance on bended knee for Ba'al. The pricked blood
in the shrines at Dan and Bethel. The 450 prophets
who dine with me at Ahab's table. The fields
full of quartered bulls. My priests will not be leaving!

Oh, Samaria, so hard it was for me to leave
my Sidonian people by the sea. Lured to the gate
like so many brides to Judean and Edomite fields
by ivory-paneled palaces, precious stones
and warrior kings. There were no railing prophets
then, just exhortations to spill Assyrian blood.

There is an ardor in my husband's blood:
he erected this capital just to keep me from leaving,
So often did I threaten it. But you, prophet,
what do you offer me? Am I some widow at the gate
gathering sticks, nothing but a stone
cruse of oil, whose son lies dying in the field?

Would you multiply my loaves to fill the fields?
Would you turn this jug of wine to blood
for me? My praises are carved on Moabite stone.
the black obelisk of Shalmaneser notes each leave
I take. Your famine will not reach our gates,
so many vineyards I've acquired. No, my braying prophet,

I am not chastened by your prophecy
that *dogs shall eat Jezebel in the fields
of Jezrael.* There is no trembling in my gait.
Seize my priests, let the brook of Kishon clot their blood,
so what! Whatever Ahab wants, I will not leave
to chance—a forged note, a word, Naboth will be stoned.

Whitmania

I celebrate Whitman's birth
by walking across the bridge named after him,
stopping by his two-story row house
on Mickle Street in Camden, New Jersey, a stone's
throw from the Delaware River, where a band of kids
gathered, gazing and pointing, poking at some body

floating face-down in the water. It was not Whitman's body,
of course, who died a century earlier, but the berth
it made in the wharf, that enthralled the kids,
who tossed sticks and flowers, chanted an improvised hymn
based on nursery rhymes and church, then got stoned
and left. I loitered back to Whitman's house,

its only visitor besides the guide who doubled as house-
keeper, who showed me the metal tub he soaked his body
in, too small to contain it, filled to the brim now with stones
saved for renovation. And a few sentimental things from birth
or soon after—christening gown, spoon, family hymnal—
quaint beside bearded portraits and folios bound in kid

skin. I once tried to teach Whitman to middle school kids,
substitute teacher, they wouldn't get the *why*'s or *how*'s
of his greatness. Why name all those things after him—
high school, hospital, hotel, wildlife habitat? His body's
buried nearby, and he's had favorable rebirths.
I'm sure we've passed, *city of orgies, walks, and joys,* cobblestones

unremoved. His mausoleum with its imported stone
seems less garish now than then, but he wasn't kidding
about his own magnitude and the secure berth
he'd hold in the pantheon. His Mickle Street house
is a reliquary for his bloated, abscessed, tubercular body
pageant. Pensive and silent I proclaim my love for him,

my unashamed, possessive, acquisitive thralldom of him,
till I get halfway across the bridge, as I fling stones
from the grave into the river. Ways to lighten the body,
I'm always seeking, like a mother dropping a kid
from her womb, how this creates an ever-expanding house
of poetry, the only thing that can sustain continuous birth.

The Idiot

I was invited to read some of my poems
at the Polish Embassy in DC,
a celebration, of sorts, of Zbigniew Herbert's
life and work, a decade after his death,
his year, the Polish Sejm proclaimed.
Of course, I wasn't the only reader

there—and one distinguished guest, who didn't read,
though he'd authored a slew of works about the *poetics*
of arms control and whose most dubious claim
to fame—lauded only, I think in DC—
was helicopters in Vietnam, the death
and destruction they brought. What would Herbert's

Mr. Cogito, his everyman say, since Herbert
often spoke through him? I dreaded having to read,
like some spokesman for so much death
and suffering, so I chose my poems
carefully, after wandering all day through DC's
museums, wary of sounding any sort of proclamation

or making any great moral claims
for poetry, though I do partly believe. Unlike Herbert,
I didn't live through war, revolt, or prison. My trip to DC
was funded, though I have, of course, done the reading.
My long trek made me thirsty, late, and poetry
was not on my mind. To keep from dying,

I'd just taken my heart meds, and in the dead
silence of beginnings I reached out to claim
a glass of juice, gulped it down, grabbed my poems,
formulated some rationale how they related to Herbert,
then recalled with horror what I'd read
on the pills—*Avoid grapefruit Juice.* Here in DC

it was bound to happen, a foreign embassy in DC,
convulsions, drool, seizures, trashed decor, I'd die
spotlighted, pathetic, the kind of scene you'd read
in Dostoyevsky's *Idiot.* As if a proclamation
had been issued, *this might be the year of Herbert,
but when it's up, there's no further need for his poetry.*

Abraham Unbound

And then it happened, the terrible stress
test: you must do this, if you know what's good
for you. Sacrifice your son, Isaac,
burn his body on the sacred mountain,
God loves pleasing odors as much as obedience.
So Abraham acquiesced, raising the knife

above his already bound son, the blade of the knife
glistering in moonlight. Halted. Like a song with its stress
on happy endings—moon glow, star shine, always obedient
to what the public craves. Relief at this good
news. Excursion into the woods, a well-marked mountain
trail that isn't an altar but a shelter where Isaac

digs into the picnic lunch his mother packed, where Isaac
pumps the groaning well till water gushes, the knife
sheathed. Then back down riprap and scree mountain
paths, exuberant, triumphal, son with father who stresses
that it was, after all, all in fun, that he—the good
father was never actually the slavish obedient

servant. Though he does suggest obedience
in keeping the whole thing under wraps and Isaac
acquiesces—fearing that he'll be branded the good
son, dupe of his father. They agree to ditch the knife,
practice ancient Chaldean techniques of stress
reduction and give a sacred name to the mountain

to quell its gossipy spirits. And the mountain
acquiesced too. It kept its secret out of obedience,
but couldn't contain itself—innumerable stress
fractures through which the fragmentary tale of Isaac's
all-too-willing-sacrifice streamed. The burnished knife
and how it almost slit his throat made such a good

story to hungry poets eager for the goods,
camped out in tents at the foot of the mountain.
That is what they wanted—no mere leap but a jack-knife
into faith. They also acquiesced, obedient
to the cover up, letting Abraham and Isaac
Off the hook: a quiz show to lessen the stress.

Task

Take some barley cakes and take some change,
and if you meet a homeless man along the way.
don't halt but pass by in silence. The ferry
to transport you across the river is there to board,
patched and pitch-coated and sea-worthy.
Its passengers resemble ghosts, but they've paid their fare

and so should you. You might think it isn't fair,
the destitute cast aside, but you can't change
the rules. It might seem to be a worthy
thing to save the drowning man or make your way
ashore to buy that lovely gown, to greet those who board
in style, but once you step out of the ferry,

and face the creatures at the dock, you'll know the ferry
is your only hope. Those cakes will be a tasty fare
for those hideous guards—just act bored,
nonchalant, and you'll see them grow docile and change.
They will no longer block your way
to the throne of the divine couple whose worthy

gift you must retrieve, more worthy
than anything you'd find above. Quickly ferry
it off and don't let hunger or curiosity get in the way,
even if these rules, too, don't seem fair
and you'd prefer to linger in their unchanging
presence. There is so little time to board,

and the prize, what's inside the tiny box, will have bored
a hole in your heart—even if you think it might be worth
it. You will only survive above is you accept change
in all its fluctuations. If you're lucky you'll meet the ferry
as it arrives, reverses course, and your trek back will fare
well. It is so easy, so commonplace to lose your way

as others have. Others who've wandered way
off course, thinking, yes, this might be a fine place to board
for a while, an eternity. And doing so, blow their return fare,
or pry open the box, thinking it will make them worthy
of lovers' desires. Or that the surface tension might ferry
them into loving arms—that longed for—preposterous change.

Why I Keep Writing Sestinas

The first sestina was by the Troubadour poet
Arnaut Daniel and immediately imitated
by a host of others, including Dante in his "Stony Lady,
Pietra." Try not to focus on the monotony
of the six or seven-fold repetition,
it's just right for a song of mourning,

dolorous, despairing, melancholy—a morning
spent with a stubbornly forlorn poet
who thinks his words deserve repeating,
which makes him (or her) no more than an imitation
of the rest of us, who think our own monotonous
lives deserve airing. We've all been betrayed by that lady

or that man, or else we've been that lady
who betrays. What's so special about your mourning
over this or that? It's all monochromatic, monotone,
without inflection, at least that's what some poets
would have you believe—and inimitable
once their special touch makes it worth repeating.

And, of course, repeating
over and over. If you think this is about some lady,
well, you're mistaken. I am loathe to imitate
anyone, by God, and when I arise each morning
it's not with the intent to sound like a medieval poet
"with a wailing and immoveable monotony,"

As though *monogamous* and *monotonous*
were homophones, a sentiment oft repeated
since the earliest troubadour poets
began to obsess over cold-hearted ladies
like Pietra. Knowing there's never a morning
when they'd awake side by side imitating

lovers, as if *intimate* and *imitate*
were also homophones. If something's monotonous,
at first (to cite a Zen saying) then try it all morning:
what seems at first mere repetition
will turn profound. Tell that to the stony lady
and perhaps she'll forgive you for being a poet.

Free Mumia Cheesesteaks

We're always extolling the virtues of Philadelphia
to our kids, who grew up hundreds of miles away
in the Midwest, so once, with a bit of time free,
driving home from the shore, we stopped for cheese steaks.
It was between *Pat's* and *Geno's,* both world
famous, but it was mid-afternoon, July 4th, fireworks

slated, and if we wanted one with the *works,*
and didn't want to be stuck in Philadelphia
traffic, we'd have to merge quickly into the world
of hunger and sloth, wending its way
around telly poles, lampposts, construction stakes
to *Geno's,* terrible choice, once we saw the *FREE*

MUMIA poster next to a *Home of the Free—*
English Only sign. Here, among working
stiff Italians who love their cops, who'd burn at the stake
a cop killer like Mumia Abu-Jamal, though Philadelphia
Police messed with the crime scene, refused to weigh
exculpatory evidence and lied. The whole world

knows he was framed. Except in this world
of skived beef, cheese whiz, nothing carcinogen-free,
where all's devoured and nothing's tossed away.
We know exactly how it works—
even as a young teen Mumia was targeted by Philly
cops, for trumpeting Malcolm X, each year the stakes

raised, his file expanded, every day a new stake-
out. "Mumia, only authentic revolutionary in the western world,"
political prisoner 3 decades on Death Row, reviled in Philly
lionized everywhere else, the empire will never set him free.
If he were to be executed, there would be fireworks.
"You can track 'em, absorb 'em, dilute 'em" put 'em away"

but you can't let 'em speak." We went away
hating the greasy, sodden, gamy, steak
sandwiches, disconcerted, taken aback by the work
undone, crestfallen in this fallen world.
There's no chance Mumia will be set free,
these days we rarely make it to Philadelphia.

House on Ashbourne Road

I lived in the house on Ashbourne Road
for two years. There, among the four of us,
I had the slope-ceilinged attic, stifling all summer,
last to move in. Most of us were done with school,
Mark stalling over a final paper on Vermeer,
Fred, locked-out of med school, helping to research

locomotion. At one time or another his research
paid us to pedal a stationary bike, and while we rode,
inserted live electrodes into our calves. Vermeer
would never consent to portray any of us
in such protracted pain—the Delft school
favoured striated interiors, spears of summer

light hitting their mark. One summer
it was Joe's raspy saxophone, next his research
into Vedanta, his chosen field for grad school.
Our house stood at the end of the road,
by a Romanian Church—its bearded priest seemed to us
the embodiment of an icon that Vermeer

would make over into a cartographer, or that Vermeer's
apprentice into a fat, smug, ruffled burgher in his summer
garden. Our heater broke after a friend visiting us
barricaded himself in our basement to research
the effect of urinating on the coils. We rode
out his madness as long as we could, law school

a longshot now, fished from a creek by the old school,
it took three huge cops to cuff him. Vermeer,
eschewed such subjects, no lightning strikes on the road
to Damascus like Caravaggio, and no summer
harvest revelry like Breughel, unless new research
finds otherwise. I was waiting tables, which to us

Seemed noble. Mark fell in love, and unlike us,
groomed himself for marriage. We were schooled
in the lesser arts, driven to the most primitive research.
We longed for a landscape, a realm that Vermeer
would ache to paint. After our second summer
the town closed off—in order to repave—the road.

The River

Orpheus gazes across the river.
He spots Eurydice sitting on a rock
on the other side, beneath a bridge
that's been defunct for ages. She draws
in grave detail the place where she came
from, before her memories of it disappear.

Orpheus forswears, frets over the disappearance
of his bride. The waters are turbid, the river
full of confusing currents, but he came
to rescue her from death, to rock
the underworld, and with his song, to draw
her back to his side. He's confident he can bridge

the infinite gap, that water beneath the bridge
will bear his grieving weight, that he won't disappear,
be washed ashore. He's seen her draw
before, the transparent facets of the river,
the gleaming, hypostatic rocks—
she often sat—on his side—when she came

to sketch. But the last time she came,
something happened—perhaps she fell from the bridge,
or jumped, pushed, bashing her skull on the rocks,
fished out by a trolling death transport, disappeared
for good, until Orpheus spotted her on the river's
far other bank. His mind at first, draws

a blank, until he recalls an old master drawing
of the River Styx where a creaky skiff came
to ferry the dead across the mist-filled river.
And there she was, deposited under the bridge
where she prevailed like a troll, not yet disappeared,
where she cleaved to the shelf of rocks

isolated and remote as an aging rock
star, all her fans gathering, drawn
to the spectacle, loathe to leave or disappear
once they discovered that Orpheus came,
prepped for adventure—all set to bridge
the gap, reverse the flow of the river.

Pomeranians

She told me she bathed her Pomeranians,
today, all three, one at a time,
the unbathed hiding behind the couch,
terrified. And once bathed, gambolling
up stairs, pattering across the hard wood.
One more onerous task to check off

the list. It reminded me of Chekhov's
tale, *Lady with a Lapdog* (a Pomeranian)
and that sad Yalta night wandering the woods,
strangers, knowing they only had a short time
together, and how the love they waged was a gamble.
Chekhov, the master who knew how to couch

the most bitter impossibilities—the empty couch,
delayed carriage, guttering candle, Chekhovian
touches, the last few rubles gambled
away as the Gypsy sings and the Pomeranian
snarls. Snow drifting, piling upon time,
they pray that something would

break the monotony—a wolf howling in the woods.
The old father, his congestive heart, slumped on the couch,
his silent mate, their neurasthenic son wasting time,
you think, oh, of course, another minor story by Chekhov,
but it's really those same freshly bathed Pomeranians
she told me about as we drove past the gambling

casino on I-75. Besides, if the son did gamble
away the family nest egg, it probably would
be Dostoevsky squandering his legacy in a Pomeranian
resort on the Baltic, collapsed on a hotel couch,
his impoverished mother taking in laundry. Chekhov
was loathe to leave Russia and the one time

he did, it was to die in Germany—to save time
his body packed in frozen oysters. It's always a gamble
to invoke the genius of Chekhov,
to venture forth into that dark inhabited wood,
to cautiously avoid all hints of the Freudian couch,
to ensure that this sestina is only about Pomeranians.

The Grey Goose

Bedtime each night, The Grey Goose
On tape for me and my two bunked kids,
then Good Night Irene, their only way to fall
asleep. Burl Ives crooning, then Lead
Belly to tenderize the tough unwilling flesh,
what's necessary to survive the day.

If I lived in the Upper Peninsula, my day
Off might be spent hunting duck or goose
Or wild turkey, unfeathering the flesh
To feast my family, make sure my kids
Grow plump and strong. Lead
The way into the dark forest each fall,

For Providence—at least since the Fall—
Does not provide, as promised, that each day
Will prove better than the last, but leads
Us on, offering the grey goose's
Golden egg, the fantastic magical kid
Offering the flay of its roasting flesh

To take the place of our flesh.
When the bird is shot and falls
From above and the kids
Go wait for it to land all night and day
they learn that the grey goose
will always elude them or lead

them astray. They will learn that Lead
Belly almost rotted in prison for slashing the flesh
Of his cousin, unlike the knife that couldn't cut the goose
After nine months a'cookin, after six weeks a'fallin.
The song is not about the day
we come to realize that our kids

Will have to accept our kidding
About invincibility, which falls like a lead
Weight, quashing expectations of a new day.
It might as well be incised in their flesh,
At the beginning of each new fall,
the string of goslings behind the grey goose.

Blue Grass (with Homage to Louis Zukofsky)

The whole neighbourhood aghast—to find the tour
bus of Bill Monroe and his Blue Grass Boys
parked in our street, banjos, mandolins, and fiddles
percolating before dawn, creeping across kempt lawns,
orbiting cul-de-sacs, ensnared in dead-ends,
disturbing everybody's rise-and-shine,

insinuating notions of hollers and moonshine
into suburb-consciousness—as Impalas and Buicks tore
up and down the street, swerving, swearing to the end
of the block, almost side-swiping girls and boys
huddled at the bus stop, bookbags strewn on lawns
recently trimmed, edged, and treated. No fiddling

around, parents insisted; it's a violin not a fiddle,
and if you don't practice you'll never shine.
Don't forget you promised to mow the lawn.
Keep August clear for your brother's tour
of Midwest colleges—Oberlin, Michigan, and both you boys
clean out the garage, I want it spotless from end

to end. Mother tethered at the end
of her rope—break out the fiddles.
Now, at least, we had the Blue Grass Boys
(Blue moon of Kentucky keep on shining....)
practicing for their upcoming tour
of folk festivals. They set up lawn

chairs and chaise lounges on the front lawn
for their impromptu concert—music without end,
as the banjo picker claw hammered, frailed, and tore
through the tune, and the high hopping lonesome fiddle,
and Bill Monroe himself and the smooth spit-shine
harmonies fricasseed by him and his boys.

It would take much more than this to make the boys
on my block drop mitts and balls, recline on the lawn
in the shade of landscaped maples, sunshine
cleaving the yards, to contemplate ends
instead of means—to hear *a round of fiddles
playing Bach,* to imagine a Grand Tour.

Spiritual Exercises (1)

after Ignatius Loyola

This is a meditation on hell
in which you will develop a deep awareness,
able to hear the wailing, screeching cries
and smell the smoke, brimstone, corruption, and rot,
to taste tears and sadness and remorse,
to touch the surrounding flames

and the souls enveloped in those flames.
Don't try to convince yourself there is no hell,
at least for now, proceed without remorse.
You won't regret this lack of awareness.
And as ripeness quickly turns to rot
don't be shocked to find the muffled cries

are all your own; a singular cry
in the wilderness, and if you can keep from flaming
out, imbibing the worst kind of rot
gut there is—on some horrid hellish
bender that distorts then mangles self-awareness,
if you think this somehow lessens your remorse,

you're in for a big surprise. Remorse
is the real killer; the blunt cry
of admonishment. True awareness
takes this into account, never flames
out, always addles the hell
you grow accustomed to, the rot

and filth. And if you think the rot
regenerates and that remorse
is majestically redeemed by avoiding hell,
well, good luck filtering out the cries
of the damned, dousing the flames
with that flicker of awareness

you had—before this exercise—an awareness
that now you might be able to. For there is no rot,
and it's only light masquerading as flame.
As for the belligerence of remorse,
what happened had to happen. So cry,
if compelled—you've managed to dismantle hell.

Spiritual Exercises (2)

after Loyola

Let's make this easy, think about the agony of dying.
Dim the lights. You don't want to see familiar objects
or people you're about to leave behind
or the disintegration of your own body,
devils and angels fighting for possession of your soul.
If you can create a mental picture in advance

you're ahead of the game, the trauma advancing,
predictably. But don't stop there, you're dying,
a ticking clock and your labored breath, the sole
sounds in the room and it seems that even the objects
sweat. Into a coffin they stuff your body
and dump it in an open grave, leaving behind

a tombstone to plant later, behind
so many others that came before. Advance
to the stage of putrefaction, the corrupt body
penetrated by agents that thrive on dying
flesh, microbes ravenous for more. Don't object
just yet, we haven't even gotten to your soul.

And though it's the incorporeal, eternal soul
you think, and though your friends stand behind
this claim vehemently, it's still a word, an object
among others, so dare them to advance
an argument by actually dying
themselves. What good is it disembodied?

friendship, fortune, health, and pleasure need a body—
yours—and don't forget, the soul's
really a Greek invention, Plato, and dying
just meant recycling, scrubbing it clean behind
the ears, uploading into fresh flesh. Think of this as *Advance
Directive, Do Not Resuscitate* over your own objections.

So you thought it would be easy to objectify
your own demise, the systematic rot of the body.
It does get easier with practice and, perhaps, advanced
age. And whether or not the soul's
departure matters. And once you've left the living behind,
will you recall more than the romance of dying?

After Petrarch's Ninth Sestina

Things were going so well, so easy and carefree,
all sunny days and breezy shallow thoughts,
no breathless sighs to speak of, I had it down
pat—no minor keys, no dissonance, my tunes
flowed, unceasing, nothing charged to elicit tears,
nothing to hint or provoke this sudden about face.

But now, all is utterly changed, I can barely face
what's slated next. I'd do anything to free
myself from the onslaught of decades that will tear
me apart mercilessly. Throughout my night these thoughts
persist—a repeated song, ever more out of tune,
no rousing finish but a flourishing let down.

Whatever could have caused me to venture down
this hostile path, anger disfiguring my face,
a trenchant jeer clashing into my tunes,
taking root, as though everything was a free
for all, and amorous, light-hearted thoughts
count no more than bitter tears.

Who can deny that love will tear
you apart, that once up, there's nowhere left but down
and that if anyone anywhere ever thought
differently, he deserves a jab to the face
and might as well believe that he is also free,
that he alone gets to call the tune.

Why did I think we'd always dance to that tune,
that nothing in the world could tear
us apart, that what I took to be her carefree
nature, was, in fact, her looking down
the pike for someone new, some handsomer face
on which to gaze adoringly. Abandon all thoughts

of happiness. It's not true that the first thought
is the best thought. Better to tune
in, turn on and drop out—it's too easy to fall for a face
like that, eyes always on the verge of tears
that seem to beguile, seem to beg you to lie down
beside her, as if she cared, as if this would set you free.

After Petrarch's 2nd Sestina

Beneath a laurel tree, she sits in its shade,
elegant and fair, otherworldly and pale,
(perhaps as cold as ice denied the sun
for months or years.) It was her lambent hair
that struck me first, then her overpowering eyes
that seemed to follow, as I wandered to the shore,

wishing desire could be deposited on that shore,
left to drift ignominiously out to sea, or that some shade
could easily be drawn before my eyes,
leaving her presence far beyond the pale
of apprehension. At least until my hair's
turned grey and I spend my days beneath the sun

chatting with my nurses, waiting for the sun
to set one last time. Even when I reach that final shore,
and neither teeth nor tongue nor ear nor hair
matters, and I'm barely a step away from those shades
who've crossed already, whose visage is so pale
they scarcely can be seen by living eyes,

I'll still be tormented by her flashing eyes
and the precious way the mid-day sun
calypsos wildly across her face. All else pales!
The only thing that's left to do—shore
up my defences, bury myself in shade
until the onslaught ends. Forget that sun-streaked hair

that brushed against my sleeve and made my own hair
tingle, or the flicker in those grey-green eyes,
penetrating into the densest shade.
My afternoons of lounging in the sun
are gone, no matter which lake or ocean shore
I find myself upon, growing up and old and pale,

unloved, forever beyond the pale
of requited love. And so I'm left to praise her hair,
and pray my anguished song reach the farthest shore,
so that strangers, finding themselves teary-eyed,
will know they're not alone beneath the cruel sun,
that others, too, long for the comforting shade.

Rigoletto's Daughter

Still one of the most heart-wrenching scenes
I ever saw (in Krakow, ages ago) long
Before I thought about having a daughter
or son. Poor Rigoletto, hunchback, fool,
toadying suck-up, traipsing behind wealth and power,
always on the outside, bullied by his enemies

real and imagined. Back then I had no enemies,
couldn't imagine what it even meant. My unseen
world consisted of guides and helpers, beneficent powers.
no dukes, archbishops, colonels, or rakes who'd long
to destroy me. No way I could be fooled
into thinking, like Rigoletto, that my daughter

was sacrosanct, easy of course, when I lacked a daughter,
when time and space, mind and body, are my only enemies.
Drawn as I was to the loony fool,
I still wanted to scream at him, don't make a scene
about her purity and beauty, before long
the nasty malevolent men in power

will kill her. You should know how power
functions, that instead of your tormentor, it's your daughter
in the sack you rip open. Barely time to long
for retribution. Now, as a father, I know my enemies,
and they are legion—the teacher, the neighbor Iv'e seen
loitering, the coach, bus driver, they can't fool

me, their aims are nefarious and only a fool
or someone without a child would doubt their power
to destroy. I map out every twisted scene,
every conceivable way he'd ruin my daughter,
the choreographer, conductor, enemies
all! And it won't be long

until I hire my own hit-man, my longing
for her safety that great—no fooling,
I'd jab an electrode into the heart of my enemies
if they prevailed, and if it were within my power
to avoid Rigoletto's discovery of his lifeless daughter.

The First Choral Ode

from Euripides' The Bacchae

The word I most love to hear is *holy*;
its open-mouthed rush of wonder like a lover's
excited exhalation above me.
Pay no attention to the King as he tears
into our sacred realm, casting insults left and right,
bad-mouthing those among us who worship

pleasure. He threatens to restrain our worship,
halt our revels, our dance, our flutes, our holy
laughter, the whole time proclaiming it's his right
to plug the flask, to snatch it from my lover's
hand and spill it. He'd rather we shed tears
instead of woes and rip the ivy vines that cover me.

He stands for everything that's alien to me:
cautious speech and harsh cold reason he worships,
enforced order, nothing felt to the point of tears.
But the gods who dwell day and night in the holy
know that a clever, controlling, ambitious lover
will always be rebuffed and never ever right.

Only men and idiots think they're always right,
forgetting how quickly life passes. As for me,
I dream of sailing to an island to meet a lover
who might be a svelte god longing for a worshipper,
or climbing to a clear mountain lake, silvered with holy
water. Who'll transport me there, tear

me away from this life of dull and dreadful tears
surrounding me on all sides, left and right,
up and down. By all that is holy
I pray for relief and escape. It's not just me,
I speak what others think, even as they worship,
praying not for health or riches but for wild love,

devising new ways of making love,
knowing that nothing will tear
them apart. Wine to help them worship,
rich and poor alike, to make wrong pain right,
and even if this seems base or common to me,
it is the only thing that's holy.

Monsieur Swann Takes a Walk at Night

Monsieur Swann takes a walk at night
along the boulevard, beneath the swelling trees.
Those few who wander past,
are barely recognizable, though a shadow
now and then approaches, murmuring a word
in his ear, asking him to take her home.

Monsieur Swann startles, having left home,
not wanting to return until the interminable night
ends. He anxiously brushes up against these words
that seem to emanate from the trees
or somewhere in the deepest shadows,
as though, in his kingdom of darkness, he's passed

the one he sought. Read *Remembrance of Things Past*
if you want to know the rest. You'll never leave home
if you do—Proust renders other prose mere shadow
language, and poor Monsieur Swann will haunt your nights
and the rest of the world will seem just so many trees
and stones that long to be transmuted into words.

But it's not only the mid-day doldrum words
that commandeer; everything in the past
that hasn't already reined in the trees,
making of them a perfect home
to keep the frightful night
free of harrowing shadows

will remain relentless in its attempt to shadow
you and shower you with searing words.
Imagine what it might be like to share the night
with Monsieur Swann—if you can get past
his foolish pretense and feel at home
in his realm and his uprooted family tree.

Don't think this is not mistaking the forest for the trees
or about the inherent murk of shadows
or the instability and fugitive nature of home.
Just utter the word
and we'll wander together beyond the past,
meeting Monsieur Swann as he takes a walk at night.

Just Like Giacometti

We see him like we want to see him,
brooding, giving birth to his own genius,
fuming, raging, lashing out, chain
smoking wild beast imprisoned
by the world, flaunting his ravishing too young
mistress in front of his careworn, suffering wife

who duly thinks it's the sworn duty of wives
to take it. She, like us, loves him
more than life itself, or comfort, or our young,
whom we forbid from becoming geniuses,
ever inventing new ways to imprison,
surrounding them with intoxicating daisy chains.

We love the artist more, the more he chains
himself to his work, his studio, makes a wife
of his sculptures, rod-impaled, lined-up like prison
bars. Only then can we truly cherish and cosset him
and get a grip on his genius,
and keep him from devouring our young.

Forget that we aspire to be like him when young,
until our first two-wheeler bike chain
jams or snaps, and we learn we lack the genius
to set it right. We're helpless while the neighbor's wife
promises her husband's help—depend on him,
the soulless handyman, your best bet to avoid prison

without abandoning the idea that misprision,
neglect, concealment, and rebellion defines young
temperament and becomes the universal hymn
that accompanies the breaking of chains.
Feel free, like him, to snag your best friend's wife,
or husband—it's all the same since genius,

presides, not gender, and it shouldn't take a genius
to recognize that *mind-forged manacles* imprison
us, and that by unshackling them, we midwife
our own rebirth, become young
enough to slip Houdini-like out of the chains.
But whatever we do, we won't blame him.

The Book of the Wilderness

When we enter, it is no wilderness.
There are posters marking the path
with pertinent information, easy bearings.
Still we quickly lose our way and blame
winter runoff, lax moral compass, inept sign
painters, and the germinating dark—

some worker who quit when dark
descended, gravelling over this wilderness.
Should we take this as a sign
presaging some unavoidable path-
ology and end up heaping blame
upon ourselves, after baring

our souls? "Seduce her, speak to her heart, bearing
her into the deep pit where only the dark
can save"—Hosea says, who's not to blame
for the leaf-mush and bottom-slime wilderness
that jinks and then confiscates the path.
Soon we encounter fellow hikers, a sign

we're not alone. They say it's a bad sign
that branches ripped your jacket, baring
bruised flesh. They point to a path
back to the lot, there's nothing to see in the dark.
Believe us, your friends, leave the wilderness
while you can, keep quiet, they warn, they're blame-

less—as if blaspheme preceded blame.
Stumps emerge from the swamp and sign
off before replenishing the wilderness,
leafless like demon children bearing
stunted fruit served up in dark
reliquaries left strewn along the obliterated path.

It is our good fortune that we've lost the path,
and no one is to blame
for driving us into the dark
wood, where everything is a sign
of everything and all bearings
are pointless, until we emerge from this wilderness.

The Middle Ages

After a while it seems pointless to enter the dark wood,
making sure to stumble upon the right entrance,
ensnared in brambles, asphyxiated by swamp
gas, on the off-chance some unworldly sacred structure
might appear—its host secretive and welcoming
and his daughter, who might not be his

daughter, leashing the hounds whose hiss
is prescient. If your venture fails you would
have lost seven years of your life. Welcome
to middle age where you're no longer entrancing
(if you ever were) where, unless you have structure
to your life, *your* every day will be swamped

by *the* every-day. Here, in the Great Black Swamp
where you dwell, croaking frogs and hissing
snakes eradicated a century ago, replaced by lawn structures.
manured fields and lit, marked paths through the woods.
Now it's all about finding the entrance
in order to exit and not wearing out your welcome.

Everyone says you should welcome
this reprieve from the fumes of the swamp,
sweetly noxious as they are. How entranced
you were when the castellan opened his
portal and urged you into the dark silent wood
to the monster whose defeat might re-structure

reality—yet this is a flimsy narrative structure,
you should heartily welcome
its dismantling. For surely you would
do all you could to avoid the swamp
of despair and the detestable hissing
crowds as you cower back to the entrance,

defeated, the magic spring's entrance
still blocked, the impenetrable structure
unassailed. As for the beast—you never wanted his
demise, you secretly suspected the welcoming
advances of the king's daughter and the swamp
of her sex. You never trusted the *would*.

The Other Side

by now he must be confused/ As to which side is which
"Charon's Cosmology," Charles Simic

It's not easy shuttling back and forth
between the realm of the living
and the realm of the dead. The line
of demarcation is always shifting,
scrunched or fractal-like, expanding out,
gerrymandered by those in charge,

a border resistant to brute charge.
If you mark the spot three times, on the fourth
it's been relocated. It's meant to keep you out,
it's meant to vex, to gall the living,
this near cataclysmic polar shift.
You'll always cross this line

in the sand without knowing and a safety line
is useless. Convicted, having been charged
with crimes, accused of all kinds of shifty
behavior now and henceforth,
forced to remain here with the living.
They shout, you've been expelled, called out

by the best and brightest, out
of bounds. Get in line
with all the rest, those who can't brook living
this way—cattle prods with their electrical charge
to keep you from moving back and forth
forcing everything to redshift.

Don't think you stand a chance of shifting
the blame. You won't get out
of this one unscathed, but I suggest you set forth
anyway, ignoring that oft-repeated line
that apparently gives them the charge
they long for, that keeps them among the living.

You, on the other hand, despise the living,
and if you could, would shift
the two sides around, allowing the dead to charge
in, and instead of kicking them out,
would straddle that difficult line
dividing the return home from the setting forth.

1968

After hasty debate we vote to bar
the door, dim lights, and shout
him to silence, the invited speaker, Vice
President of the college. His topic: *Nathan the Wise,*
18th century German play by Gotthold Lessing
Our behavior, though wretched

is cribbed from Franz Fanon's *Wretched*
of the Earth, a work meant to bar
further colonial subjugation, his lesson
for Africa. "Fanonization" we call it, shouting
Stop this war! Stop it now! feeling wise
in our protest against the worst of vices,

war-mongering, child-slaughtering, and vice-
presidential nattering. Enough to make us retch.
We think ourselves wiser
than any working man sidling up to a bar
in our college town and shouting
at the tv news, cursing for more, not less

bombing and napalm, teach them a lesson
they'll never forget. The college vice-
president shrivels under our shouts,
hounded until conceding his own wretchedness,
musing, I'm sure, about Scotch at the wet bar
board meeting, his disquisition on *Nathan the Wise*

scrapped. He planned to reveal that wisdom
is not some elaborate shell game Lessing
staged. And then we theatrically bar
the door, squeezing-in like a vice.
In the play, the Jew Nathan makes his wretched
plea for tolerance as the Sultan and Christian knight shout

and threaten. And we, impatient, shout
him down. Thus, lost to us, Nathan's wise
parable—the loving father who gives each of his three wretched
sons a pearl, not knowing which is less
genuine, admonishing that each should live vice-
free and vie for righteousness, that raised bar.

Clavdia Chaucat's Chest X-Ray

Clavdia Chaucat's chest x-ray—
There's nothing more intimate, the plate
of her damaged lung, her gift, her soul,
placed in your hand after a carousing sweet hour
of bliss, And your one last look at her Kirghiz eyes
before she leaves the sanitarium for good.

Tuberculosis is no longer the good
Romantic disease it once was. X-rays
replaced by MRIs, cat and pet scans, the eye
penetrating disintegrating flesh, no more plates
of alpine beef and cheese served on the hour,
as the cold damp mountain air restores your soul.

It takes someone like Clavdia to rouse your soul,
to seal you off from the world below for good.
Who'd want to return to a realm where hours
tick off and a holocaust of the sun's rays
douses reason. Think of her hair done up in plaits,
dark tendrils, and the warp and woof of her eyes.

If nothing else you'll forget you're an "I,"
forget distinctions between body and soul,
consciousness shattered like a flung plate,
nothing there to shriek bad or good.
Take it from her, affix it to the wall, her x-ray,
its corrosive spots, gaze upon it for hours,

for now she is yours and no longer ours,
dearest Clavdia with the Kirghiz eyes.
While you're at it, catch some rays
up here on the mountaintop deck, sole
recipient, since all the others, good
compliant patients, scrape clean their plates.

and prattle about spotless x-ray plates,
miracle cures, healthy glows lasting hours
and how intractably good
they feel. They look directly into your eyes
as though they were interrogating your soul,
the whole time discounting the truth of the x-ray.

Sestina With a Line From Major Jackson's
Reverse Voyager

I never met your "Mrs. Pearl, a grandmother, a domestic,
thirty years boarding SEPTA early mornings"—
though I grew up in a suburb at the end of the line,
where weekdays old women from North Philly walked
down the block, trudging back up, weary and burned
out, to catch the spasmodic, sluggish "A-Local" to Broad Street,

Poplar, Strawberry Mansion, or Columbia, the street
where after King's assassination, riots displaced domestic
tranquility, and the neighborhoods burned—
around the time you were born. For weeks, mourning,
displaced minding kids, cooking, cleaning, and walking
the dog. My parents protested the whole system, their line

old-time socialist—even as they moved into the red-lined
suburb, mortgaged a house on a still-unpaved street,
no butcher, baker or barber, no tailor or tucker in walking
distance. Only unlandscaped lawns grazed by domestic
sheep and mounted red-clad fox hunters on Sunday mornings
and the fall stench of leaves and chopped brush burning.

And next door, my best friend and his maid Edith, Crisco burning
in her pan, delivering up fried chicken we'd line
up for, even as it sizzled. On her break each morning,
Bronze Thrills and *Jet* and chitchat out in the street
with her compatriots we called maids, domestics,
girls, though they had their own kids, grandkids, walked

their own crooked miles for decades, so we could walk
straight, unimpeded, avoiding the sting and brunt hard work,
recreating a sort of dreamy domestic
living room scene, reifying the Eisenhauer-Kennedy line.
Where Coup de Villes and 98s drifted down our streets,
excursions into unfamiliar territory, on Sunday mornings,

proving and disproving King's claim that Sunday morning
was the nation's most segregated time. Side-walk
barrier, barricade, bulwark, rampart, dead-end street,
worlds further riven, as my neighbor's clothing store burned
in the North Philly riots, losing his whole fall line.
Blessings for Mrs. Pearl, grandmother, domestic.

Sestina as Kabbalah / Kabbalah as Sestina

When you attack a city, don't destroy the trees,
commands the Bible. Why would you—anyway—
cut off your food supply? Fruits and nuts are not human,
they're innocent, sinless. Good advice: leave
the date palms alone. In the Psalms, we learn
that studying the Torah slakes your thirst like water,

as if the coolest, purest water
seeps into the roots of a stream-side tree,
and that the more we study and learn
the more we discover the ways
of delight, become those burgeoning leaves,
fruit of our roots and branches. In the human

realm, this translates the Torah into human
wisdom, sustenance and water,
so the Angel of Death will leave
the innocent alone, allowing its trees
to thrive, which is God's way
of preserving the Tree of Life. Thus the learner

moves through the sacred text, as Rabbi Lerner
advises, fully aware that the human
condition is one of brokenness, weighed
down by evil deeds, sunk in primordial waters,
out of which a single tree
can barely rise. You must abandon, leave

the swale, what you've been as lief
to do thus far. You've learned
all you can there, stripped the tree
of its bark, remained all too human,
the wine turned back to water,
and everything is standing in your way.

Enter another wilderness, push your way
through the snagging tangled skein of leaves,
trudge through the treacherous waist-high water.
There is no other lesson to learn
that the only way to bridge the human-
divine divide is to become the cosmic tree.

Flame

Once when Rabbi Ben Azzai sat amid his students,
they noticed a circle of flames dancing around him
as he expounded. Terrified they went to their master
accusing the Rabbi of delving into secret
forbidden realms. Called to explain the fire
the Rabbi denied making utterances

that might arouse demonic forces, utterances
he knew would endanger his students,
lead them to presume their own souls were fired
up and ready to fly. So Ben Azzai recited the hymn,
As wax melteth before the fire... It's no secret,
the wicked perish in the presence of the Master.

The Rabbi knew that mastery
comes from linking together words and utterances
from different realms, uncovering meaning secreted
behind each story, remaining a perpetual student,
searching for the fleshy skeleton key always eluding him.
It's only the words that detonate, catch fire,

reveal heretofore hidden passages. Play with fire—
you don' t always get burned, you can learn to master
the heat. The flames never touched him,
no one ever heard him utter
an unkind word to his students
and so they learned to keep his secrets.

The Rabbi's words themselves rejoiced, their secrets
unraveled, dancing as if on fire,
quavering, lapping up close to his students'
ears as they strained to master
audition—preparing for their own.
They had never before heard a hymn

so sweet, so delectable, spilling from him.
This they learned was the only secret
worth knowing—how their utter
delight, like a refining fire
incinerating the cruel task-master
within, could redeem both teacher and student.

Rasalila Dance from the Bhagavana Purana

Nothing can keep them away, once they hear Krishna's
flute and rush eagerly from all directions,
earrings jangling under the copper moon, as they abandon
cows and cooking fires, infants and husbands, even lovers,
leaving cries and untended flames, threats and accusations,
their dress and hair in disarray, eager to feel his caress.

Each one convinced she alone will get to caress
the beautiful, long-haired Krishna,
until they meet his terrible accusations—
"Go home right now, listen to my directions,
your families need you, the ones you truly love.
The night is full of ferocious creatures, abandon

this madness, think of those duties you abandoned—
please your husband, suckle your babes, caress
instead your aching parents, no matter how bad at love
they are. This is the only way to please Krishna."
They are devastated by the unexpected directions
and shudder at his cruel accusations,

bewailing, Inconsolable, until one of them accuses
the beautiful god of abandoning
his own true nature, mouthing the directions
of some lesser god, of withholding his caresses
just to toy with them. "O Krishna,"
she cries out, "what kind of lover

seeing the vermillion powder on the breasts of his beloved
would not be moved, realizing his accusations
caused the teary kohl of her eyes to smear it. O Krishna,
for your sake we have sacrificed and abandoned
everything, is it too much to desire your caress
when all you do is gaze in another direction?"

So she begins to walk, crestfallen, in the direction
of her home, her deep and arousing love
dismissed, forced instead to caress
her own crossed arms. Will her accusations
make Krishna relent? Will he abandon
his cruelty? You know the true nature of Krishna.

Songlines

*The man who went on a Walkabout was making a ritual journey. He trod in
the footprints of his Ancestor...singing...—and so recreated creation.*
                    —Bruce Chatwin on Australian Aboriginal spirituality

The world does not exist until you sing
it into existence, though you are not the first
to call it forth. Others before, back
to the very beginning, have freed it from its mind
prison, given it life, only to have it disappear,
again, like a baby's favorite toy

hidden by some teasing adult. That toy
is gone for good—there's wailing till she sings
and coos when it suddenly reappears.
It's like she's seeing it for first
time, not as some shadowy image in her mind
but shimmering and vibrant, unwilling to back

down or retreat. It's time to draft Rilke back
into service—Apollo is no toy
deity, and to enter his Temple requires a mind
that's undefiled and a hunger to sing.
You must set aside your youthful soulful anthem first
and let your show-stopping belting disappear

so that an exalted breath can appear
like some god sighing in a back
antechamber for the very first
time. Don't let others toy
with your world or degrade what you sing,
or urge you to keep it locked away in your mind.

Begin to excavate, make sure it's mined
and brought to the surface, appearance
corresponding to reality. Then can you sing
what others have sung, wander anywhere and back,
your path like a musical score, a wind-up toy
unwinding, an extravaganza of first

causes. Your ancestors were the first
to create, and you must always keep that in mind
when you replicate, as with a magic toy
recreating what would surely disappear
or disintegrate, hauled off on the back
of an ancient beast—if you fail to sing

My 6th Grade Teacher

Mr. Barren
chose two boys each week
to swim with him at the downtown Y
back when it was male-only—to swim nude
in the cool chlorinated waters amid schools
of old men, their buoyant testicles and laps

without end. One girl got to sit on his lap
each Friday for the pep-talk he called Barren's
Bulletins (or bullets) advice to succeed in school
as he pointed out the strong and the weak
among us, and how the ancient Greeks wrestled nude.
No one thought to ask him why

he did these things. Being chosen for the Y
swim or his held-hand—our own judgment would lapse
like Sadducees, who sent their sons to the nude
Greek gymnasia to exercise, or fleet-footing across barren
patches of land—anything to avoid the end-of-the-week
Sabbath rites and the effete Talmudic schools

hosted by Pharisees, who scorned schooling
unless it was Mosaic Law. Upsilon, or Y
in ancient Greek denotes, for mathematicians, a weak
number, an orphan child, one you might cradle on your lap.
We learned language games early in Barren
Hill, where we lived, till our town fathers renewed

that old link to the Revolution, renaming the nude
hill after the Marquis de Lafayette along with our school,
where the butterfly-stroking-ex-Olympian Mr. Barren
continued to teach us. You might wonder why
we put up with him, even lapping
up his put-downs throughout the school week

when it was meant to keep us weak
and pliant, and if he'd had his way, I'm sure, nude
for indoor recess. And those endless laps
around the honeysuckle-strangled school
perimeter for punishment. And why
I miss the time I spent with Mr. Barren.

The Seven Signs

for JSK (1919-1998)

She already exhibits four of the seven signs
of imminent death, my sister reads the Xerox sheet
the social worker sent. Too late—the kids
lunge for the almost fumbled phone, pile on top
of the baby. The oldest uses the cord for double
Dutch, my *shushes* and *shutups* provide the chants.

I try to convince my sister that there is no chance
of reversal, that the deep and glorious sign-
off her friends encourage her to expect will only double
the letting go. My mother's white as a sheet,
barely eats, but throws her legs over the top
of the bedrail at night, dangling them like a kid.

And when denial strikes, we both know I'm kidding
when I bring up my father's blind belief in chance
over necessity, what almost took him to the top
of science, the atomic blast he could have designed
but didn't. Now he tears her soiled sheets
and measures detergent in calibrated beakers, double

strength to stanch the stench of death. Double
her pain meds, the hospice says, no kidding
around, this stuff you see oozing on the sheet
is her flesh melting off her bones, and the deep chants
abrading like a Russian hymn are her rendition (sign
six) of her dead answering her call, flopping on top

and shaking what's left inside loose, leaving the top
free to glare at us who stay, redoubling
our efforts. What strange and eerie kind of sign
was it when we talked on the phone? Even the kids
grew quit, the baby gnawed the nipple, my last chance
to hear her voice—before the winding sheet

gets wound, its starch crackling and crazing like sheet-
rock in the early stages of demolition, about to top-
ple under the Renovator's blows. No chance
it will be left standing in the end. Doubly
strange for us offspring—parents retracting into kids,
meeting ours along the way, flashing signs.

Listening to Messiaen's "Quartet for the End of Time" at the Toledo Museum of Art

The audience across from me composed of Franz Hals
burghers and their wives, ruffled collars and coarse
snoods, who tip their stern heads in rapt
appreciation, as they recognize bird songs
from picnics and country outings within the music.
They all seem ready to flash open their black

gowns to reveal gleaming trumpets cinched to their black
undergarments and blow furiously in this vast hall,
so all four players might cast aside their sheet music
and instruments and dance—with the rest of us, of course.
Though afterwards they'd have to renounce this song
and replace it with silent motionless rapture.

And thus, Messiaen, burghers, all of us, wrapped
and enfolded into eternal blackness
beyond the reach of any song.
For now, though, in this peopled hall,
where measured time proceeds on course,
we let it maneuver through us, this music

composed in a Nazi prison camp, music
that today keeps the museum guards in rapt
forgetfulness of their duty, to kick out coarse
sound and movement, to keep the black
clad musicians undisturbed, to usher from the hall
those mothers whose infants' songs

won't be bottled-up. Messiaen's song
only partially pleases the burghers, for whom music
is only good when it draws huge crowds into the halls
of commerce, and goods can be sold and wrapped.
They emerged after the catastrophe of the Black
Plague and thrived, unmolested in their lucrative course

until the early 20th century. Of course
collapsing when fascist marching songs
and swastikas and black
armbands cuffed and plundered music.
For now, there's only this rapturous
Requiem, unconstrained in this or any hall.

About the Author

Leonard Kress has published poetry and fiction in Missouri Review, Massachusetts Review, Iowa Review, American Poetry Review, Harvard Review, etc. His recent collections are *The Orpheus Complex, Walk Like Bo Diddley,* and *Living in the Candy Store and Other Poems.* He has also completed a new verse translation of the Polish Romantic epic, *Pan Tadeusz* by Adam Mickiewicz. Kress teaches philosophy and religion at Owens Community College in Ohio.

Made in the USA
Middletown, DE
17 February 2021